THE BIRTHDAY of THE DEAD

P O E M S

THE BIRTHDAY

of

THE DEAD

Rachel
ABRAMOWITZ

CONDUIT BOOKS
& EPHEMERA

ISBN: 978-1-7336020-7-5

Published by Conduit Books & Ephemera
788 Osceola Avenue
Saint Paul, Minnesota 55105
www.conduit.org

Book design by Scott Bruno/b graphic design

Distributed by Small Press Distribution
www.spdbooks.org

Cover images: James Ackerman, *The Infant Beggars,* courtesy
the Library of Congress; *Kropsla [Lactuca sativa var. capitata],*
MPM.HB.04260, courtesy The Plantin-Moretus Museum, Antwerp,
Belgium; Dried flowers and leaves, Depositphotos.

CONTENTS

for

MICHELE

Severed Head of a Giant 40,000-Year-Old Wolf Found in Russia

I don't speak her language, but I see her tongue,

pink-tipped and red underneath, underworld
brawn. I will her into my house, but she paces
outside the door and makes a sound like fire in her throat.
I have only so much law. I have only so many days
to her cold eternity. She has been waiting in the rime,
though her coat is thick enough for this new earth.
I watch from my window steam rise from soft tissue
and have no spells for such a skull, such promising teeth.

I can only transform numbers into things:

This many hairs make a braid you can hold
in your hand, this many years and you will never see
yourself again. There are depths some can sound, but what reaches
for you there will be made of flesh so terrible
you would cut off your own to be free of it.

Vantablack

All the animals you know
will die. You set food out for them anyway,
let the oily seeds fall among the fiddleheads to be ground down permanent
   as bone.

The forest fills and unfills, drops itself down root tubes and turns to dark lace.
One undoing: leaf to sparrow, ghostly star.

Or there is no death.

Or the face death sets sucks
light like that special paint, the one that plunges and harms.

They painted a barn that special paint, and the barn disappeared.

I Go Wandering Inside My Head

alone. At the gate of my head: a bull the color of hot tar

on yellowing paper. He ignores me, chews the perpetual grass.
Beyond the gate is a scape like the moon. It is not a known moon,

nor of poetry. It is a red moon, and subtle, and I walk
backwards to see where I have been. The gravity here

is the weight of an apple on the highest branch.
When I try to catch the apple as it falls

I am inadequate as a pebble-hued moth.
Slim as a coin, the moth makes holes so great whole

empires fall through them over and over. Let me return
to the civilization whose god is a sunfish, flat as a palm.

There my hands are nonsense: I just wave them around, astonished
by their disobedience. They draw only the bull, its face the face

of a heart that has seen itself, and walked through its halls all the same.

My Heart Is a Horse

-hair cushion. My heart is a black
hut where the moon gets in through a hole
no bigger than a dime. Like the moony face
on the wall, the petals of my heart stretch so hard
they fall like galaxies. O tiny red-legged jewel,
carnelian on a rugged beach where the only flowers
come from the sea. O molehill, how you
appear, heart-like, against the green fields.
How the apples of this orchard open their jaws
and eat every horse they see.

Anniversary

I married the last spoon
in the drawer, the one with a chip
in it from when it got caught
in the disposer and whirred
and whirred the sound that hell
must sound like, until someone turned it off
        (it wasn't me)
and a quiet descended like lint
to the floor which reminded us
of the vows we had made to each other,
the spoon and I, which were rushed but referenced
the violet light of morning cradled in sterling
        (everyone wept)
        (especially the other spoons, which were occupied
         in puddings and white sauces and reflecting
         the ceiling from the counter)
and that quiet was like the inside of a spoon
where not one day has gone by that I do not think
of my imperfections, a thousand thousand
points of light—

Once I Lived in a Great City

laid out to bring the sun into itself at certain times of the year, and
    everyone at that time
of the year left their offices made of straight lines of glass and heathered
    upholstery soft

as a fawn in spring, and left the construction sites that would soon
    sprout more offices and left
the diners whose insides are cushioned in brown vinyl, as it is written,
    and left their tender

fruits to the flies and left their shining children to wander around
    the fountains that reminded
the children of ancient Rome, which they remembered all of (heat
    pooling in a courtyard,

lazy smoke from a burnt ox, a freshwater pearl in a ditch) and left their
    spouses holding
the car keys but soon the spouses also left and for several minutes
    everyone forgot how to drive

anyway, and the sun in the city entered the streets with shared purpose,
    with a pure, unerring
heart, and even the concrete warmed with the memory of the beginning
    of the universe,

which was silent, imagine:

The Source of the Nile

Before the voyage I left a houseplant
just for a time but the seeds tipped out
and now among the Ginny leaves
sprout the tenderest most anonymous grass by mistake

you have to get to the root
and I don't know where that formula begins

some wind-caressed breadbasket of the Mediterranean
or north among the furred and busy lichen

before the Messiah was even a twinkle
in the galaxy's sucking emptiness

before the translation of nothing and now

that the houseplant is in my white stone house
the grass reaches, unnamed, to the potted banana
palm in the yard which is lonely

as the Nile on Mars

Sonnet: Introduction

I must have had a mother. I must have had
    a hat, and then given it away, upside down,
    so that someone would be compelled
to fill their head with crocuses. I must
    have seen how golden the moon
    appears to a virgin of Demeter, wreathed
in glowing wheat, betrothed to dirt. I come
    from a village accessible only by boat; you can see
    how the heat clings to me, how from my ankles
dangle netted glass, blue lobsters, pieces of kindling,
    four tamed crickets ready for circus life.
    Sweet hedge maze, verdant under every planet,
I will show you what the center is made for.
    Here is my hat. Something has to change.

Each Meal Here Was Once Alive

I hold my head on its column of clay   beads still
                as a ruined field. I trick the dumb
        dove down   from the branch she stresses
even in her hollowness. In this garden,
        ants the size of dinner plates from a distance.
Each meal here was once
            alive, you say,
and press your ear to the tomato vine
                to count its rounded   heartbeats. I envy
        the penmanship of sweet peas, the vigilance
of rosemary, cabbage leaves   marked like astral
            maps by moths. Figs swell and split—
                a cicada shedding its skeleton.
When you hold one out to me
            I drive my thumb into its seeded throat.

Your Life in Art

Unlike the living, the dead tell you when they are tired of you. They make endless pots of wedding soup, and oil their breasts in the moonlight, and ask what the tides are doing, and the rhododendrons. Wardrobes awash in green silk, blackberries tucked behind their ears, they will nod when they would like you to pack up your red pail of sea glass and take the sun away. How easy it is to talk to the dead. I have a standing appointment. We lunch in the old ways, pretending to our great estates. The sea rattles beneath the earth, and we turn our eyes to one another. We talk of Bruegel and his winters, though here it is spring, and the bathers down by the rocks feel only an occasional gust. There is no plague, and when the sun dips behind the beech trees, and the sandwiches, light as foam, are all gone, I walk back up the drive, and feel the magnets in my blood like ancient hands pull me toward the dirt.

The White Goat

I would like you to lend me the sound of its bell,
though I cannot pay you back

even in grass for the goat, because
there is nothing to balance

that valance. Just the interest would drown me:
leagues of Carthaginian wheat and yellowed stone.

A bell is made of: 1. a bell yoke or headstock, 2. canons,
3. crown, 4. shoulder, 5. waist,

6. sound bow, 7. lip, 8. mouth, 9. clapper,
10. bead line. The imagination rounds out

like a mountain swallowed by its earth. I am reading
this to you from my sound bow, my bare bead line.

The bell is a bead that hangs from the goat's throat.

The More I Give, the Hungrier They Get

Great silos of seeds that, if planted,
would cover the earth end to end, would grow

in the places savaged by fire, mud-drowned,
blasted with an age-old atomic thrum.

The seeds are tumbled ruins on the beach,
drops of magma frozen to a high sheen.

Smooth as doves, my slippers. At the window,
the agate eyes of the cat twitching with murder.

The faces of this earth are terrible: a pear
orchard, the desperate mountain clouds,
the tropic undergrowth of treacherous green.

The birds here are brown and gray, though
their thoughts are of what the moon does

after it leaves the tide to its muttering foam.

Two-Headed Tulip

Green-Wood Cemetery, Brooklyn

Of course dead things bring
      up the best flowers.

What a merchant wouldn't give
      for your heart-bulb, pleated
as a new onion in a brass-hinged box

marked *Future*. What titmouse
      wouldn't pause in his survival
to be lifted on the electricity

      of the sight, an instant evolution
on this patch of grass. Even the dead
      are reaching like roots for your name.

The Name-Giving of Athens

If I am a brick baking on the surface of the sun,

      then you are a tiled pool, aquamarine, no bigger

than a table for four. On this table are oranges,

         such that the sun shows you, although in the field

           only plums grow every few years and by surprise.

Mice also in the shorn fields, great kingdoms and revolutions of mice.

        The sea's feathers closing upon each other.

     If I am a clay jar of water and a drowned

fly, you are the obvious olive tree and its small

        brown bird who is your only sorrow.

Kairos in the Garden

My child's dark curls: this god of opportunity.

      The house lifts us into the jewel-green yard
full of bully jays and petal-light finches. The tongue

      of a breeze on my arm, on my ankle,
while my child spreads her fingers over

      the house and blots it. The sun, she is.

      The sun a hot fist hovering there.

A Japanese maple darkens its purple,
      though elsewhere rocks give up old themes.

      My child and I say goodbye forever.
What faith: the orange blossom tree against
      a pastoral sky. My child, whom

I do not have, leans into the grass
      to bury a marble in the center of the earth.

The Appian Way

The pink-and-white house and I
get to know each other. I place it
on a hill suspended above ordinary cypresses,
where a stream goes about its lapidary business.
The house gives me a white cat
with eyes green as Alexandrian marble,
and I bring the house lemons sometimes,
and we eat them with salt because
we are alone. When it rains,
I swear, the house sways
like a lesser boat. In summer,
infantries of ants storm the blue
bowls full of plums, and the house
and I count and count.
Some months the house
tells me the truth: we can
not go on forever, and how
its beauty dredges up
in me whatever it is
that makes men thunder
down wondrous roads
toward that which
can be made to kneel.

The Age of Prophets

is over again. You spread time

over your own wingspan, then file off

    the end of your longest finger's fingernail to show
    how briefly our bodies have lived. Mostly amoebas through

the arms, the torso, an unremarked stirring

        near the wrist. The first giraffe to dare for an upper leaf,

    warm eyes slipping into phalanx
        formation or surrounding the skull

    like sentries. Meteors brush by us as in a crowded bar,

skin on skin as far apart as reams of empty space, casting off
the same dust and ice I'm told we're made of. What luck:

    to meet now, in a land of occasional cleanliness

        and safety, as when the audience, emerging
        from the dark cinema, stops to watch

a single monarch butterfly zag across the street.

    No one knows if it's real, or if it's one that just pretends.

The Puzzle Monster

Francis Bacon, Three Studies of Lucian Freud, *1969*

Thousands of eyes are roaming

around. The cage demarcates

only the cage: unhappy ape, praying

for everything, museum-ache zinging

his whole spine. Such velvets and golds for living

through the worst. *There is nothing else,* says the ape. *Eat!*

Flowers bloom on his skin. We scoop

up the deep reds and purples of the insides

of meat, of fruit: blessed be the monster

who made you, who makes you still.

Dead-Color

I had just finished painting the still life when it began to move, which
  in truth

    it had been doing all along, and at once I found I had been doing
      great violence

all along the seams of tulips, the dusky grapes who sang to the
  bats outside,

    the lemon-sized body of a bird who lobbed herself at the window,
      and both I

and the painting began to rot like a cantaloupe, that is to say from the
  inside and with temerity,

    and holding the painting to my softening body I saw that garden
      that spends its life

open-mouthed in jungle increase, in the biblical work of unguarded heat—

In a Past Life

Tell me what you're married to and I'll tell you the book
to read to get out of it. Tell me which of these pet store fish
you're most attracted to and I'll tell you that most likely you
were a peasant in a former life, hundreds of years ago,
in a valley that looked up onto the lush expanse of baronial
wealth you served. I'll tell you about grief. I'll tell you where
they've hidden the pigeon babies, sickly, Jurassic, valentine-pink.
What do you want to hear? I carry this cheap pennywhistle
in case of a request on the wind. About grief: let me tell you:
it's an oil slick in winter in a parking lot next to a frozen lake
where men drill holes in the ice to get at the flesh beneath.
Over time you get used to that cheap song. Cleopatra splintered
into many souls. There is an explanation for everything.

Chat-Renard

It is the halfness that confounds.
Amalgam of hot

and heather, slinking through
the landscape like a numen,

soft, with provocative teeth. What
stories they have for you: babies snatched

in the candled night, returned
and shifted behind the eyes, mewling new

at darkness and asleep forever.
That coiled bridge between worlds:

Blood, spinel-dark, underneath.
What enters their dreams: hind legs quick

and keen, balancing in a shaft of light—
one eye illuminated, one hushed in the gloaming.

Octopuses Invade Welsh Beach

An octopus walks out of the ocean and
    dies on the sand, gasping a terrible wet human
gasp, eyes fixed on horizon, strange
    land, water line, the salt of a particular death,
and then another comes, until there are twenty.

We approach them one by one, a receiving line,
    and their tentacles curl and wave, tighten and drop.
There is nothing to be done. They are escaping
    a zone so barren it is called a zone.
It is hard to breathe where they are meant to breathe

    so they have come to where they cannot breathe at all.
It is better this way, each brain tells the other:
    Let us meet, like a noble army, our death
on a beach in the night, let us haunt it with our final shapes.
    It is quiet except for this strange sighing—

    The hearts blink out, and the useless shell
        is set on the sand like a plinth.
    And then we, with our piteous one heart,
        say nothing, and the stars say nothing but make pictures
        and we wait for the tide, and know less and then less.

Animal, Vegetable, Mineral

My death shadows the lower land; I know it.

I have little to offer: insufficient coinage and clothing, glittering silt
from the shallower puddles. I can dig. I can see over the scrub pines for miles,

find my way among dandelions pelt-thick, peer
through thickets dense as first-told fairy tales, darkening backwards.

At dusk death perches in a tiny silo window,
or is junked like a tanker at the edge
of a hot ocean. So many other hands pull at it,

but it is mine and I—its. The vulture below my eyeline
pays out her debt of love to the roadkill in every place.

An entire deer asleep in a ditch, suspicion of red. Perhaps this place
was once underwater; it will be again.

Ice in summer from clouds, I swear, heavy as earth.

My Death Is a Rose-Apple

and sometimes the green of paint under a tree
where the artist has decided to capture
this field and its cow and love in her festival dress.

My death looks humbled by the flowers in a painting,
or by the red hat of a politician's wife. This red hat,
my death says, is like all the flowers in one, as reflected in her face—

the politician's wife has been dead for a long time, and knows what my death
is talking about, and even now is dying in a painting.
A rotting purple fig on the table under the vase of tulips

is an exercise in the perpetuate afternoon. I try to follow
what my death is saying, but sometimes I drift off and about this I feel guilty,
because really I should listen but O

how I would like to touch my death's hand to my face.

Divination

In the dream I woke from last October, there was moon gruel for everyone.
Flowers in everyone's sleeve, peeking red and blue out

like a warning. You asked if you could have a plum
from the new-bud branch. The first one, you

said. As you were turning into sweet herb
I felt assent was paramount. A single scrap fell then

at your feet. The poem had meanings
I could only brush against. You read it to me in your lunar voice

despite the cracks in your shoes and the skin blotching under
your leaded makeup. When your horse passed by, I was sure

to wave at each horse and that you in truth were looking.
You were going on a blind date, you said, and I said

watch for the moon beneath the trees. A person could utterly blossom.

I Don't Know Any Gods

My child arrives in a monastery
    far from the sea, her eyes
domed as bulbs in wet dirt. To reach this monastery
    I walk for years: lyptus wood for feet, the ragged
twin suns of my knees rising and falling. My hair, grown large,
    houses generations of spiders,
although they only speak to me when I bring
    my head close to the ground: *your child*
will be ravenous as a quarry, unadorned as a cliff,
    holy as an impassable shoal.
I don't know any gods. *Ill-favored,* they call in voices
    like a thousand masts splitting at once—

So He Thought

Women turn into lakes all the time.

I rely on the old tropes: one hand outstretched,
the other clawed around a spear, the arcane

forest floor silenting each footfall, each
minor note. Sparrows that were women,

these oaks, of course, and would you be surprised
if this deer tick, this sprouting fungus,

had a human song inside it? Now that I am
this watery shape—bring your face closer.

River yourself beside me, intransitive. I lied: you
will know me by the faulty joy of foxgloves,

whom no one will touch, and who grow everywhere.

The Sharpest Milk Knife in the World

Elsewhere a man
or woman makes
a knife out
of milk and it
is the sharpest
one of its kind what
can be said
about the sharpest milk
knife in the world is
that when applied
to any vegetable
the vegetable
sings and its cells
leap up to embrace
the milk
knife and the milk
that is the knife under-
stands this foliate
language and for once
there is harmony
and even outside
the cow stares over
the sill of the kitchen window
and pauses in her
lament for the world
of dew

I Was Carrying Supplies Back Up the Mountain

When I heard the white birch on the other side of the mountain
Give over and split right down the middle like paper
(If you can imagine)
And the birds unsettled
In other parts of the mountain forest,
And the mountain somehow took note
And shifted. Maybe this meant snow,
Or fog, lurching towards the muted valley
To be pushed up again by a doomed, unseen hand.
Maybe the valley would fill
And the echo would drown and reflect instead the trees.
And I carried my supplies the rest of the way.

This Is My Day for Crime

For forty-eight days it rained inside the battlement.
I held the baby that was given to me

by an attendant, and when he cried or smiled
I took that to mean that the rain would stop,
but every time that silence grew like the silence

of a leaf. The attendant heaped snow
on a platter and recited a poem about the snow

and a moon and the plum, but this was the Daylight Chamber
and crime has no beginning or end. In fact
a frog had jumped into the fire and was burning away.

A Fable

I am a monster with a great sunken heart.
      I am a cat with a baby in its mouth. A bad baby. A monster baby
        born underground.
          I watch the earth being born and then slipping
            underground. At the center of the earth
is a hot heart that pulses and pushes
      and in this way I am a heart. My baby is a coiled heart of danger.
        My whole little baby. I am only a small monster.
I am a pit in the earth filled with clay where nothing can grow.
      Someday the earth will eat the baby and   the baby will eat its heart.

Hell

When I was famous I held my heart in my hand like a plum.

Hell is a beautiful plum.

The saddest picture I ever saw was of Hell's aching shoreline—
Two swans on the horizon.

Come visit me here. My house is made of whalebone.
My white tent. My foreigner, my plum, my single colorless gong.
It is said that the seabirds come often to the garden.
Hell is sweet comb.

I have asked you to visit.
Half song, please visit.

I will wait in the landlocked sea which is not Hell as you would expect.

The Second Dream of Happiness

I drew a picture
of a house
this morning peering
from the chalk
board phantom
roofed with an angle
no one has measured
leveled light fell
on it so clear it
was like a snow
day and I
knew that on that day
there would be people
in my drawing
mirrors not
just empty
circles

A Conversation

The moon does not
want to be touched.

How do I know?

The goats this morning
bludgeon each other
and then roll in the daisies
singing their childhood songs.

The moon wants

(it has said to me)

only to go swimming,
and here is a lake
like an opal opened
from its cave.

Come closer, moon.

No gods prowl
these shores.
Nothing mudded
or poison-fleshed.

I will teach you
to float, to hold
your celestial

breath and feel
the water close
over you like an eye
closes, and everything

will go on growing
but for a moment
like the top of a breath

will pause and either
go on or perish.

Love Letter

I'm an unsmall rabbit at dusk
under the pine tree.
The moon is not out
but I do not know the moon anyway.
As the light fades
I find a good blossom.

> *

I am a serpent-head fish
on the table of a small house in the woods
because there is little time left in the day and someone
must remove my bones and it will not be me.

> *

I have a new teacher.
She is a white shell on the beach and sometimes
she is a rotting crab leg on the beach.
Often she is just a rock,
or a rock that is more bone than rock.

> *

I am a strawberry, like you.
But I have been shaded from the sun
and am malnourished
and will remain here
under this leaf.

> *

Oh!
How like the sun you are—tell me everything you know.

A Hunger

It was a deer leg in a tree.

    Bent like an architect's compass, hinged to meet

        the forked branch, also thin, also leafless, still in early spring.

Hoof up, looking nothing so much as a goose head, a graceful

    upward angle which meant something had gone horribly wrong

        in the knee. And it had: gnawed at the joint, ball and socket

naked and dry, though shin and foot were still furred, looked warm.

    Someone had found it, of course, or torn it

        away from the dogs, that mass of practical fury. And then hung,

or hanged, or draped, or set it like a gear into the tree.

    As if the world were made of nothing but hunger.

        Imagine the rest of the body deep in the woods,

already swarmed in its second, heaving life.

The Birthday of the Dead

The theme of this party is truth irreducible—
silver streamers suspended from a tall tower.
The musicians, sleeves billowing, play hits
perennial as the hellebore. Anyone who comes to this party
in the clearing should take the proper precautions:
Wear white, or if not white, red. It is the birthday of the dead,
who have brought their postcards and jewels.
Who has made this blood soup? Poor goose, lured
with rich scraps. We have charted the migration patterns
of these flocks, years of planning for the birthday of the dead—
It is in this clearing that we pull them apart.

Poem [Under the modern regime of beauty camouflage, everything about woman is detachable except her ears.]

I have one of those removable complexions.
I molt blonde hair, shed my automatic teeth

and discard my mechanical eye. I am older than hieroglyphics;
I gain every lap. I walk the plank,

pearls in my heels, swirling like Ophelia's resentful drain.
I accent like a fig, rot as bouquet, fly at the blooded meat.

I am your tulip bulb and its papery dress, lifted.
I am cooked, early in the day, and set

to ooze and plump. I am a wand, a cup, the clack of wristbone
on wood. I have one of those foldable complexions

you can carry in your handbag.
I peel back my sockets, show the swift and dazzle

of my inner mud. I gum me, fooling. I have one
of those sinkable complexions, swaying to the bottom,

current-sick. I am young as an ambush.
There will be a camouflage for every ill.

Love Song for an Enemy

Old patient song! I know what suit you wear,
whose mother you were, where

you've hidden the pearls.
O to be your burning rib, your heartthread,

a black braid—Remember! You are one
of us! Though the city is far and the season

green. Or, if you like, light haze
around the skull, the ancient spellings

of vestigial bone. You have tried to be bad,
living beneath the world. I never think

of you. Tell me the truth.

I never think of you.

The Orange

To look or to listen? Or to touch, to offer
the soft-downed small of your back, like a canvas,

to the blood-rush of both gentleness
and pain, the same blood blooming

against the boundaries. Of course what I touch
is space only, the brain filling in because

it wants to live. It digs because it wants to live,
covers because it wants to live,

but as the orange on the counter begins
to whiten and fuzz, I don't think you want to live.

You don't want to die either, because I have seen you
look at the orange and its death

with something beyond fear
or revulsion: a decision.

You look at me, deciding. To touch, then, to watch
oneself in another's hands, to feel, in this moment

of decay, beloved or useful.

Drosophila melanogaster

Drawn to the *sparkling clarity*
of Heinz's apple cider vinegar
three fruit flies have given their lives

in my house for their love
of ripe death, three—
let us say it—emissaries of light, tiny

zooming angels, sent by life itself
to shepherd this banana
into its afterlife, and once

in the Vatican I, like an ant, thought
about my wobbly
insignificant things, about the Pope at night

pressing Athena's cold cheek, or lying
on his back in the map room adrift
on approximate seas, or lifting a rusted breastplate

from its subtle hooks and clasping it,
flaking, to his own breast.

Outside, the sun
does its hot starry thing and the wind
wrests water from a cloud

and drops it on the earth.

Traité d'Ostéologie
drawing of a female skeleton, 1759

I am a village, tiny in the distance.

Come to the village, I will bake bread, I will
not breathe too much. My feet are small.
My ribcage is as narrow
as a fist. I grow bluebells

along the village walls, I am allowed to,
they are mine for the while.
Sometimes I am a cat in the shape of a woman,

I slip around doorways, unfurl
the insides of mice and birds, a knitting
I know. Watch

and be amazed.

Lost Angel Head
after B. Catling

When I returned from the cragged valley,

there was only: butterless dinner, winecasket sunk,

praying mantis in dark glass jar (eyes like operas)—

I was, then, nothing-legged! The clouds: taut with purpose!

The hedge maze thickened around my once-mended brow,

toads utterly everywhere envied the valley's robin's-egg straw hat.

(The valley and I walked arm in arm, believe me, until out of my sleeves
came nothing again.)

Men of Poetry

Only the ghosts of nightingales beneath the floorboards—
do not weep. With every step you do not crush
the fine bones of their bodies so they sing out
the alarm. Men cannot be stolen. They walk away,

their robes silent in the blue night. I cut them like seeds.
I cut them like teeth. Like teeth they ache through one's body,
wend their way around nerve and bone. In the great hall
the bones pile up, eye sockets smooth as an egg. The eggs

of the native quail tremble on each plate, tremble
all the way down the throat and set the body to trembling.
Oh, to watch one's companion weather this. It is like
slicing out one's tongue and feeding it to a god.

Lives of the New Saints

O how it spills from me, this light, not from my pores,
      from holes smaller than that, so great is the rush of light

that it makes its own particle-sized holes, or wave-sized holes,
      whatever. I am made of light, hallelujah.

You would think these holes, made by this particle-wave,
      whatever, would hurt, but like any good saint

I do not complain of my injuries. I would take more, more!
      Give me the spear! Give me the mace, the ax, the broadsword,

the Catherine wheel spinning in a lake of fire, so above mortal pain
      am I. So bathed in light that even the men who come to spy on me

bathing in light in this clearing in the woods
      are blinded and forevermore led by goats.

So blessed by light am I that when I bring my sword down
      on soft noble throats I feel only the breeze

in cities I have not yet looked upon in my wrath of light.
      My light swims back to me as to a black hole,

unbearable in its need. Watch me spin to the center of the earth,
      where light breaks into liquid, finally wave, finally furious.

Origin of the World

A night sow chews the flesh of a peaching moon. The moon,
    through the flickers
of prehistory, sings to its adopted children, the daffodils. Daffodils sink

    into the muscled earth, shoots
jawing with the worms. The worms
know several languages badly, and often the shade

of their feelings—chiming, goat-
smelling, witness, braid—goes untranslated. A goat
    eats an accidental worm in love
      with a nettle. The nettle has loved before, but not in these colors,
        not with this exquisite

    reckoning. The planets know only this music. The sun watches
      everything like a crocus.

My First Disappointment Was

that they weren't pears, blushed undersides
loopy for the ground, sack-heavy and pulpous-

sugared. They were apples, severe, green-sick,
too high up to contend with dirt.

The sky didn't make a fuss, although in that moment
I wanted to die, or to be a cloud. The river at the edge

of the orchard, such as it was, tumbled its rocks smooth
as fruit in low spring, and the cold it drew from the center

of the earth seeped into the apples, which looked
at us in our laced clothes and red

shoes, with our hands ringed through each other
and our mouths softening, and willed us away

from that place, though we stayed
until our arms vined around and around.

An Elephant Man Lives with the Mirror
from Francis Bacon's Studio
after B. Catling

Watch me in my stripes tonight. Watch

my fingers crack an egg into a vase,

candled and shivering. Here is the real

horror: the house swims away like a gnat in milk

from my body, like the middle

of the night it is. My brain dark

as bread. Oh, these? I've been collecting pond

branches, they eat their hearts

out for the moon, don't you agree?

The mind is a bone fruit, don't you agree?

Have a simple shout, as from behind

a painting. Let me speak plain: the Lord

does not quake only the beastly. Believe me:

I have cradled my own waxen head like a ship, like a woman.

The Horse

And into then a carriage with no sail.
Thoughtful I wandered, reins in hand,
exhaling as best I could, considering.

My friends think I'm right to watch the night's
portrait carefully as I can, barking aloud and jotting
its *scuro* into my hushed book. Driving by the park:

The trees slice the sky into dark blossoms,
filament, encore. Don't set your best orchards on fire
or drown your nightclothes or sing to me.

I've seen more in the capsized moon than dark-motored history,
and when my horse gets thirsty, I lead him
to the damp earth. He knows what to do.

The Future Has an Ancient Heart

All the peaches go bad at once.
    My riders enter from the left, single trumpet—

Decomposition!—battered as a tulip. Feast this:
    A cow's heart enters a thousand underdirt maws, tongued

arterial, a kine adrift. What was once wound is now a waiting.
        Lord, what I would not give for extinction, for the desert of
          our rivered youth—

        What cup is this. What white bird, plump as a thought,
eats from my trough. I have nothing but horse hair

            for my dowries. I give birth in cathedrals of hay.
    A wet new bird, I do not leave the earth.

What a Terrible Magician

I am. I can't even turn the canary's heart
    into whispered black ash, a poor early diamond.

        Every time I try to double the snow
on the forest floor, the trees slink away and the light is the light

      of some dumb Tuesday in late March, hardly
        enchanting. The moon drops one of her lucent veils

onto the head of my demon, who wails
    with such desire that I shut him in a cave.

      I give him a lamp and a chair and a narrow bed,
and when he calls down from the mountain

        I forget the color of snowdrops, the feel of two
   identical birds, hearts like nothing at all.

Another Fable

The petals of the dogwood
are white as a church.
I break them apart one

by one, and from afar
they look like they have flung
themselves down. In the grass,
an ant walking through the blades

finds herself suddenly shaded,
and chooses not to be afraid.
The shred of petal that has fallen

upon her reminds her of a house
she visited long ago, and though
there were no crumbs in those
sheets she had felt the same melancholy

of late summer where heat ripens
itself out. The ant has lived
for thousands of days, and is

in love with the dogwood tree,
who surrenders itself like a saint.

Aubade, Hwy 12A

The river broken with ice. A tractor rusts out beneath a wilting roof,
a banana peel blossoms from a dirt-scabbed snowbank, and although
    from a distance

the trees endure an individual dignity, up close their arms are
    uncomfortably thin.
In the pinched hedgerow: a male scarlet tanager, bright as a
    crushed berry.

Dogs bore golden holes in the frozen embankments. White as salt meat,
    the road splits
in its lanes despite the dark patching, squiggled as writing. I don't know
    if the small, furred

bodies on the side, opened by speed and metal, are worse now because
    their stillness
is the stillness of the hillside. The river is endless: it ends at the bottom
    of the sea.

ACKNOWLEDGMENTS

Some of these poems or versions thereof have been published in the following journals:

American Poetry Review: "Severed Head of a Giant 40,000-Year-Old Wolf Found in Russia," "Vantablack," and "Chat-Renard"
Beloit Poetry Journal: "My Death Is a Rose-Apple"
Green Mountains Review: "A Conversation"
Greensboro Review: "Each Meal Here Was Once Alive"
I Wave Composition: "I Was Carrying Supplies Back Up the Mountain"
jubilat: "My Heart Is a Horse"
Literary Imagination: "A Hunger"
Seneca Review: "A Fable," "I Go Wandering Inside My Head," "Your Life in Art," and "Once I Lived in a Great City"
Sprung Formal: "Dead-Color," "The Puzzle Monster," and "The Dream of Happiness"
The Threepenny Review: "Octopuses Invade Welsh Beach"
Tin House Online: "In a Past Life"
Transom: "Hell," "Love Song for an Enemy," and *"Traité d'Ostéologie"*
Tupelo Quarterly: "I Don't Know Any Gods," "So He Thought," "Sonnet: Introduction," "The Source of the Nile," "The More I Give, the Hungrier They Get," "The Age of Prophets," "Love Letter," and "Poem [Under the modern regime of beauty camouflage, everything about woman is detachable except her ears.]"

ABOUT THE AUTHOR

Rachel Abramowitz is the author of the chapbooks *The Puzzle Monster,* winner of the 2021 Tomaž Šalamun Prize (forthcoming from Factory Hollow Press in 2022), and *Gut Lust,* which won the 2019 Burnside Review Prize (Burnside Review Press, 2020). Her poems and reviews have appeared in *Tin House Online, The Threepenny Review, Seneca Review, The Kenyon Review Online, Crazyhorse, Tupelo Quarterly, Prelude, Oxonian Review, POOL, jubilat, Sprung Formal, Transom, Colorado Review,* and others. She is a graduate of the Iowa Writers' Workshop and the University of Oxford and has taught English Literature at Barnard College in New York.

CONDUIT BOOKS
& EPHEMERA

OTHER TITLES FROM CONDUIT BOOKS & EPHEMERA

The World to Come by David Keplinger

Present Tense Complex by Suphil Lee Park

Sacrificial Metal by Esther Lee

The Miraculous, Sometimes by Meg Shevenock

The Last Note Becomes Its Listener by Jeffrey Morgan

Animul/Flame by Michelle Lewis